# Cowley East Oxford

## Past & Present

MALCOLM GRAHAM &
LAURENCE WATERS

SUTTON PUBLISHING
OXFORDSHIRE BOOKS

Sutton Publishing Limited
Phoenix Mill · Thrupp · Stroud
Gloucestershire · GL5 2BU

First published 2002

**British Library Cataloguing in Publication Data**
A catalogue record for this book is available from the
British Library.

ISBN 0-7509-2761-5

Typeset in 10.5/13.5 Photina.
Typesetting and origination by
Sutton Publishing Limited.
Printed and bound in England by
J.H. Haynes & Co. Ltd, Sparkford.

A cricket match at the Magdalen Ground, *c.* 1820.

# CONTENTS

Cowley Centre nearing completion, 1964. (*Newsquest (Oxfordshire) Ltd*)

# INTRODUCTION

Oxford is known throughout the world rather more as the seat of an ancient university than as a city of great diversity. Tourists flock to see the area west of Magdalen Bridge, the heart of Oxford University, which was famously described as 'the Latin Quarter of Cowley' at a time when the Oxford motor industry was enjoying huge succes; an E.H. Shepard cartoon depicted dons filling their mortarboards with money from Lord Nuffield's (motor) horn of plenty. Even now, when Oxford is a medium-sized city with a second university and a varied economy, the very name still seems to conjure up a mental image of dreaming spires and sunlit quads peopled largely by dons and undergraduates. Of course there is substance behind this image. The university city has a stunning architectural heritage, and in spite of extensive development on all sides, its setting is still remarkable and precious; here and there, you can still lose yourself in past centuries. However, this is only one aspect of modern Oxford, and a short walk across Magdalen Bridge brings you to another Oxford, less picturesque perhaps, but with a completely different historical perspective.

This book looks at the area south-east of Magdalen Bridge which extends from The Plain through St Clement's and Cowley to Blackbird Leys. Historically, this large area was entirely outside the city limits, and even St Clement's, an extramural suburb by the twelfth century, only became part of Oxford administratively in 1836. Cowley St John, the Victorian suburb of East Oxford, was added to the city in 1889, Cowley itself in 1929 and Blackbird Leys in 1957. Until the nineteenth century much of this land, even in St Clement's parish, was undeveloped, and Cowley Marsh was quite literally marshland where snipe flourished; Oxford Road used to be called Pile Road because the highway across the mud had to be raised on wooden piles. Cowley Field, a huge area extending from Cowley village to The Plain, was agricultural land criss-crossed by some forty-seven footpaths until enclosure in 1853. Extensive tracts of farmland survived around Cowley village until the 1920s, and Blackbird Leys took its name from an old farm at the heart of the estate.

The progress of urbanisation in Cowley and East Oxford reflects the growth of Oxford since 1801 when the city had a population of 11,921. This figure rose to 27,843 in 1851, 49,336 in 1901 and 98,684 in 1951; taking student numbers into account, it now stands at about 141,500. With expansion on this scale, suburban development was inevitable, and the area south-east of Magdalen Bridge has proved particularly attractive. St Clement's and Cowley St John accounted for nearly 30 per cent of the city's population in 1901, and about 40 per cent of today's Oxford residents live in the area covered by this book. This is due in part to the lie of the land, since the Thames flood plain restricted development to the south and west of the city, but did not affect East Oxford. No single landowner was able to influence the building of Victorian East Oxford as St John's College did in North Oxford, and developers laid out many streets between The Plain and Howard Street in a decade or so after 1853. The population of Cowley parish was already growing by 1900 as people moved to cheaper properties beyond the city boundary, but in the twentieth century the career of William Morris, Lord Nuffield, was the crucial factor in creating a huge demand for housing in and around Cowley. In 1948 Thomas Sharp reflected ruefully that 'the great Nuffield works are an extension of a shed in a back garden. The Pressed Steel works are an extension again of those'.

Nineteenth-century prejudices helped to shape the character of East Oxford. Middle-class folk looking for a suburban home generally looked to the hills or to well-drained land such as the gravel terrace in Oxford extending north from St Giles' towards Summertown. Their homes had to be well-located in relation to the city and uncompromised by the existence or even the threat of poor quality development and polluting industry. Cowley Field was next to the socially mixed area of St Clement's, and there was a strong suspicion that its clay subsoil made it unhealthy. Christ Church anticipated that the area would be filled with small houses, so it planted a screen of trees along Iffley Road to blot out the development before it even began. Doubts were even expressed in the 1860s as to whether Cowley Road was a suitable place for a workhouse. In fact, effective drainage made East Oxford perfectly healthy, and some middle-class villas were built in Iffley Road, but to the Oxford elite the area beyond Magdalen Bridge tended to remain unknown territory. In a sense, this ignorance eased William Morris's path in the 1920s, since he could swiftly create a huge motor industry in Cowley without incurring the outrage that had greeted the Great Western Railway's proposed carriage works in Oxford in 1865. The area was outside the city boundary, invisible from Magdalen Bridge, and what happened there was not initially of great concern. In September 1931, two years after Cowley had been incorporated into Oxford, an intrepid journalist from the *Oxford Mail* visited 'the more populous outlying districts', like an explorer travelling into the unknown, and reported back, almost with incredulity, that new housing estates were being built all over the place to cater for workers from Morris Motors and Pressed Steel.

As long ago as 1893 East Oxford was described as 'a kind of separate town' detached from the city centre, and the same can be said of the wider area today. The flood plain of the River Cherwell provides a physical barrier, and all traffic between the old city and the newer housing areas to the south-east is channelled towards The Plain and Magdalen Bridge. Rising traffic levels led to the widening of Magdalen Bridge as long ago as 1882–3, but the only twentieth-century improvement to local communications was the building of Donnington Bridge in 1962. The Christ Church Meadow Road (1940–66) and the Eastwyke Farm Road (1968–72) were controversial road schemes that would certainly have improved communications, but both were rejected because of the huge environmental damage that they would have caused. Since 1973 both City and County Councils have tried to restrict traffic in the city centre and to encourage the use of public transport. In 1999 High Street was closed to most vehicles during the day under the Oxford Transport Strategy and, despite regular bus services, critics argue that this has reinforced the isolation of Oxford's eastern suburbs from the city centre. Better communications might have reduced the isolation, but the large communities east of Magdalen Bridge have generated many facilities of their own, and the cost of travelling into the city centre from the remoter suburbs is one good reason for taking advantage of them. The completion of the Oxford bypass in the 1960s perhaps diminished the city centre as a focal point, and the development of Cowley Centre, later followed by large retail outlets on the ring road, attracted custom away from the shops in central Oxford. With rising car ownership and frequent buses to London passing through Headington, Oxford railway station no longer has the drawing power it had for earlier generations. The city centre may still offer employment and recreational opportunities, but many people living in Cowley and East Oxford have all they need closer to home.

In the nineteenth century St Clement's and East Oxford provided convenient and comparatively spacious new houses for people who had previously been packed into courts and alleys in the city centre. Some were able to better themselves because of higher or more regular wages, while others were literally forced out of their old homes by commercial or university development and had to look for cheaper accommodation in St Clement's side streets or the remoter fringes of East Oxford. The area also became home to many people from the countryside around Oxford who came to the city in search of work, such as the widow Eliza Haynes of Horton-cum-Studley who moved to Magdalen Road in 1898 with seven children, getting a job as a domestic servant. Few people in the area were well-off, but most were self-sufficient, and they struggled to preserve appearances. Until the twentieth century Oxford's economy was heavily dependent on providing goods and services to the university; wages were low and vacations were a time of unemployment. The expansion of the motor industry between the wars soon exhausted the local pool of unemployed or irregularly employed people, and Cowley attracted a host of new migrants from depressed areas such as South Wales. Arthur Exell, for example, joined a hunger march from Pontypridd in 1928, found a job when he reached Oxford and eventually got work at Morris's. In the postwar years an African-Caribbean community developed, drawn to the area by the promise of work on the buses, at the car factory or in the National Health Service. Albert Stewart was a typical newcomer in 1954, leaving Jamaica to become a bus conductor in Oxford. Asian immigrants from the Indian sub-continent and refugees from Idi Amin's Uganda added to the diversity of East Oxford from the 1960s.

Cowley and East Oxford have therefore grown by attracting people from further and further afield; they have also continued to expand with the rehousing of people from city centre properties to Rose Hill from 1934 and to Blackbird Leys from 1958.

In the last thirty years the sheer convenience of much of the area has made it more attractive to professional people, and growing numbers of students now occupy many of the single-family homes. The area has changed radically and it will continue to evolve, but with events such as the Cowley Road Carnival there is no doubting its present vibrancy.

## THE PHOTOGRAPHS

The oldest pictures in this collection date from the 1820s and 1830s, before the age of photography, but the pace of change has become so fast that some of the 'old' photographs were only taken in the 1970s. The comparisons between old and new are like a balance sheet, showing both profit and loss: profit in the survival of odd pockets of countryside, the retention or restoration of historic buildings, the clearance of unhealthy or sub-standard housing and the modernisation of existing properties; loss perhaps in the apparently needless destruction of fine buildings and the replacement of the unique and local by the mundane and commonplace. Deciding whether the account is in the black or in the red is very much a personal judgement. Wherever possible the current photograph has been taken in the same location as the original one, but the Cowley Centre, dropped into the heart of the old village in 1960–5, obliterated the historic street pattern, making exact comparison difficult at best.

The book is arranged so that the reader begins at The Plain and examines St Clement's before exploring Cowley Road as far as the bus garage in chapter two. The trip along Iffley Road in chapter three includes diversions into streets in the East Oxford heartland before continuing to Rose Hill. Chapter four is a linear journey along Oxford Road and Garsington Road to the former Pressed Steel works, now BMW's Oxford plant. Chapter five covers the area north of Oxford Road, providing an armchair tour from Barracks Lane through Temple Cowley to Hollow Way, Horspath Road and Brasenose Farm. The last chapter explores the site of Cowley Centre and the centre itself, old and new, before travelling through Church Cowley to Blackbird Leys.

# ACKNOWLEDGEMENTS

Most of the old photographs and other images are from Oxfordshire County Council's Photographic Archive, but we are very grateful to Jeremy Daniel and Newsquest (Oxfordshire) Ltd for permission to reproduce their photographs identified in the text.

# 1

# *The Plain & St Clement's*

St Clement's Fair, *c.* 1910.

A countryman with livestock for the Oxford market passes old St Clement's church shortly before its demolition in 1830. The toll-house beyond the church was built in 1818, and travellers are stopping at the gate to pay their tolls. Away to the left, beyond the children playing with a frisky dog, there is a glimpse of the house owned by wealthy coach proprietor Richard Costar. He had an entrance on either side of the toll-gate so that he could always avoid paying tolls.

Pulling down old St Clement's church left an open space that soon became known as The Plain. The churchyard was retained for many years, and the gravestones were only removed in 1950 when The Plain was converted into a roundabout to improve the flow of traffic. Mature trees and attractive floral displays help to raise the spirits at this often congested spot.

The Plain from Magdalen Bridge, *c.* 1870. Two figures below the table of charges on the toll-house enjoy a quiet spell at what must sometimes have been a hectic spot. Beyond the retained St Clement's churchyard with its mature trees, High Street St Clement's curves away to the left, while the Cape of Good Hope pub on the right marks the beginning of Iffley Road.

Cyclists make for Magdalen Bridge as two of Oxford's buses approach The Plain. The toll-house was pulled down in 1874 and it was replaced in 1899 by the Victoria Fountain, designed by E.P. Warren and built as a belated Diamond Jubilee tribute to Queen Victoria. A new Cape of Good Hope replaced the old one in 1892, and early nineteenth-century houses (left) gave way to Magdalen's Waynflete Building in 1961–3.

The landlord, W. Burgess, and his employees pose outside the Cape of Good Hope pub on the corner of The Plain and Iffley Road, *c.* 1890. The Oxford end of Iffley Road was built in the 1770s as an improved approach to the new Magdalen Bridge, and the Cape pub soon occupied this prominent site; it was probably so called because of its peninsular position at the tip of the then undeveloped Cowley Field.

The Pub Oxford from the corner of Cowley Place. The Cape of Good Hope was rebuilt in 1892 as part of a scheme to widen the entrance to Cowley Road. It was designed for Morrell's Brewery by the local architect, Harry Drinkwater, and included, at the rear, a first-floor stable with ramped access. The pub was briefly known as the Hobgoblin before being renamed.

Oblivious to the threat of atomic bombs, passers-by enjoy the sunshine outside the York Place Municipal Restaurant in July 1967. York Place was named after the 'Grand Old' Duke of York (d. 1827) who was Commander-in-Chief of the British Army, and two early nineteenth-century houses are visible above the word 'restaurant'. The Municipal Restaurant, opened in 1944, was one of a number built in Oxford to provide cheap, wholesome food during Second World War rationing.

The Municipal Restaurant served its last meals in 1971 and, after some delay, Anchor Court filled the gap in the street frontage in 1983–4. Built by the Anchor Housing Association, the building provides ground-floor shops in St Clement's Street with flats above and behind the street frontage.

Crowds fill High Street, St Clement's during St Clement's Fair, *c*. 1910. This local fair, first recorded in 1723, was held a few weeks after St Giles' Fair in late September and remained a small-scale attraction with a few sideshows and perhaps a roundabout in the yard outside the Old Black Horse. In Victorian times the entertainment sometimes extended around the corner with a greasy pole contest at The Plain and donkey racing in Iffley Road.

The Thornhill Park and Ride bus passes the same spot today. No. 27 St Clement's Street, the furthest part of Finders Keepers, has survived from the earlier view; it was rescued from dereliction in 1983–4 in a scheme which included the gabled property next door. Increasing traffic put an end to St Clement's Fair between the wars.

Wash-day at Yew Tree Cottages, *c.* 1935. This group of twelve three-storey houses was built off Penson's Gardens in the 1860s and each house had three rooms, one above the other. Between the rows, the low central block provided the occupants of each property with a toilet and washing facilities, but their only garden and drying space was the area between the access pathways and the front doors.

Yew Tree Cottages were demolished in 1935, and the site is now occupied in part by this row of public toilets in Penson's Gardens car park. The remaining houses in Penson's Gardens were demolished in the 1960s, but a street nameplate survives at the narrow entrance from St Clement's Street, and the man in this photograph is unconsciously following its still-defined course towards the River Cherwell.

Cars parked in Caroline Street, June 1972. Slum clearance had left only a few houses, and, on the right, the former St Joseph's Roman Catholic School. The street probably owed its name to the popular Queen Caroline, wife of George IV, who died in 1821.

The surviving stub of Caroline Street from Alan Bullock Close, a development of graduate flats for Oxford University built in 1976. Older buildings fronting on to St Clement's Street survive at the top of the street, and, behind the lorry, there is a glimpse of Stone's Hospital almshouses, established in 1700.

The Victoria Café on the corner of High Street St Clement's and Boulter Street, *c.* 1910. This building and the adjoining Mission Hall were erected in 1886–7 to bring the church into the heart of the community. The Victoria Café had a temperance function, challenging local drunkenness by providing recreational opportunities away from the many pubs; a cycling club was linked to it by 1893.

Fresh-air fiends no longer dominate the upper floors of the building, and a church bookshop now seeks to feed the mind rather than the body. The Victoria Café continued in business until about 1937, and the shop became a Gospel Book Depot in 1948; it has been St Andrew's Bookshop since 1991.

Howsham Place off Bath Street, *c.* 1935. Each of these early nineteenth-century houses had just a small front room, a tiny and very low scullery with a slanting roof and one bedroom. They were timber buildings behind their rendered façades.

Today's 23–4 Bath Street were two of the terraced houses that brought people back to this formerly overcrowded part of Oxford in the 1980s. Howsham Place was demolished in 1935, then warehousing occupied the site. The postwar clearance of many other local properties left the area in a blighted condition by the end of the 1960s.

Nathaniel Whittock's engraving of about 1830 showing two gowned figures outside the Oxford Baths. The baths, which gave Bath Street its name, were designed by Thomas Greenshields and opened by 1825. The promoters hoped for a fashionable clientele and made a virtue of the building's comparative remoteness by stressing the value of the exercise that would be expended in reaching it.

The secure entrance to housing for St Catherine's College, built at the bottom of Bath Street in 1970. The Oxford Baths comprised a large oval bath, two fives courts, a Turkish bath and dressing rooms. They never achieved high social status, and gave way to housing in the form of Bath Square in 1881.

An empty pram is the only evidence of human life in New Street in about 1935. Nos 7–9 New Street were two-storeyed brick houses from about 1820, similar to many others built at the time in St Ebbe's, around Gloucester Green and in Jericho. The bay-windowed properties in George Street, the modern Cave Street, were later houses built on a site that was still undeveloped in 1850.

The street pattern preserves a degree of continuity in a very different environment. Houses in St Clement's No. 9 Clearance Area were pulled down in 1935, and the others went in postwar redevelopment schemes. The new houses in Cave Street were part of the renewal of St Clement's as a residential area in the 1980s.

Wilson Place, a small square of brick houses at the top end of George Street, St Clement's, *c.* 1935. No. 5 had two rooms on each floor, but families at nos 3 and 4 had only one main bedroom, having to use the landing as a second one when the need arose. The black brick pavement in front of the houses, added in the late nineteenth century, would have represented a considerable improvement on the original conditions.

A small block of flats behind properties in London Place now occupies the site of Wilson Place. The old houses were demolished in 1935, and like other St Clement's people who were being rehoused at the time, the residents were moved to a new council estate along the Marston Road.

Wingfield Street from the Cross Street end, July 1972. It was originally Dover's Row, built by the local builder, John Dover, in the 1860s. Respectable folk were soon complaining that it was a haunt of undesirables, and the Oxford Cottage Improvement Society demolished the row as a slum in 1909, built these plain terraced houses and named the street after the society's founder.

The old road surface of stone setts with a central drain now comes to an abrupt end. The Oxford Citizens' Housing Association, successors to the Oxford Cottage Improvement Society, built Wingfield Court across the site of Wingfield Street in 1977. Two shoppers are heading for a hidden footpath which maintains a link with nearby Glebe Street.

London Place from the foot of Headington Hill, *c.* 1926. Tall Gothic houses of the 1880s in London Place were set back from High Street, St Clement's behind an irregular group of mean properties. A trough in front of advertisements for the Oxford tailor, W.E. Fayers, and Margett's hats gave horses the chance of a refreshing drink before attempting the pull up Headington Hill.

The buildings in front of London Place were cleared in 1927, widening the eastern end of St Clement's Street. The improvement also provides a much better view of an architecturally varied terrace that features tall Gothic house of 1881 near Cherwell Street and three-storey Classical properties of the 1820s, masked by trees, at the other end.

Brick terraced houses of the 1820s in Cherwell Street, September 1971. The three-storeyed houses, nos 16–20, boasted a hall, two living rooms and a back lobby on the ground floor with three bedrooms above. The back lobby provided dedicated space for cooking and washing, leaving the back living-room free of the usual cooking smells and steam.

Cars have multiplied and redundant chimney-stacks have been removed, but the scene is still entirely recognisable. Cherwell Street benefited from a changing official attitude to inner-city housing and from the ever increasing attraction of living in convenient central locations. Opposite these older houses, council housing of the 1980s replaced Minty's furniture factory.

Undaunted by nearby cattle, residents pass up and down the avenue to St Clement's church in Austin & Son's 1857 engraving. The poor condition of the old church and the rapid growth of St Clement's in the 1820s encouraged the then curate, John Henry Newman, to build a new place of worship on a larger site. Designed in a neo-Norman style by Daniel Robertson, the new church was built between 1825 and 1828.

More hemmed in now by mature trees and apparently out in the country, St Clement's church is in fact a lively centre of worship for this decidedly urban parish. Criticised originally for looking like a 'roasted hare' or a 'boiled rabbit', the church is now a listed building.

The Elm Tree pub and former Palace Cinema from the corner of Jeune Street, July 1974. An earlier Elm Tree pub existed here in quite rural surroundings by 1839. The present building was designed by Henry Hare, architect of Oxford Town Hall, and was opened in 1899. The Palace was a cinema between 1912 and 1938, but it had previously been a theatre; well out of the way of the proctors, it seems to have attracted a fair number of rowdy undergraduates.

Blackwell Publishers now occupy the former Palace Cinema and have made a feature of the attractive frontage. Next door, Mab's dress shop has given way to McLean's Mirrors. The Elm Tree pub, another of Cowley Road's listed buildings, has just been refurbished.

Cowley Road east of Pembroke Street, St Clement's, 1900s. Many Cowley Road properties were built as houses, but the street became a major shopping centre for the growing district attracting, for example, a branch of Lipton's national grocery business. The houses on the left had resisted conversion to shops and retained their front gardens, while the road itself offered idyllic cycling conditions. (*Jeremy Daniel*)

Cyclists now have to share a much busier Cowley Road with motor vehicles both moving and stationary. Houses beyond what is now called Rectory Road (left) lost their front gardens to road widening in the 1930s. The most obvious change on the right is the replacement of the distant Cowley Road Congregational church by Tyndale House in the 1960s.

Cowley Road near James Street, c. 1910. Shop units occupied most of the front gardens on the right, and Radbone & Son's grocery shop and post office was on the corner of James Street. Cowley Road Congregational church, built in 1869, towers above the other buildings, and the tiled roof of Cowley St John Boys' School can be seen on the corner of Princes Street.

The widening of Cowley Road over the years meant that front gardens were lost and shopfronts were pushed back. The shops on the right clearly lost a lot of selling space when they were forced back to the building line. The New Inn, built in 1916, partially hides the former boys' school, now East Oxford Community Centre, but Tyndale House, now used as offices by Oxfordshire County Council Social Services, is the most striking alteration.

Two little girls watch Samuel Grafton put the finishing touches to a Diamond Jubilee statue of Queen Victoria outside 145 Cowley Road in June 1897. Grafton was in business as a sculptor and monumental mason from about 1872 to 1903, and his commissions included carvings for the widened Magdalen Bridge and for the chancel of SS Mary's and John's church.

Grafton's house and adjoining properties on the corner of Union Street gave way to a branch of Barclays Bank in 1930. Amid all the banking rationalisations of recent years, Barclays closed the branch and the Children's Rights Development Team of the charity Save the Children now occupies the building.

The Oxford Co-op delivers bread to Union Street using a new Morris 1-ton lorry, 1924. A board attached to no. 11 was a modest advertisement for Richard Pocock, a local basket maker. The small terraced houses in Union Street were built in the 1860s; the street took its name from the nearby workhouse of the Oxford Poor Law Union.

No sign of a Hovis delivery at no. 10 today, and the fire hydrant plate has been moved from the wall of the house to the front garden wall. Sash windows have been replaced and Velux windows in the roofs next door are evidence of loft extensions for more living space.

Catering for people on the move; Wiggins & Son's premises at 159–61 Cowley Road, *c.* 1906. Wiggins' were established as carriage builders in 1867, and the business adapted readily to the craze for cycling that offered a new freedom to many people in East Oxford as elsewhere. It provided a riding school where you could learn to ride a bike or perfect your roller-skating technique. (*Jeremy Daniel*)

Tesco's now caters for busy people by opening for twenty-four hours a day. Wiggins' continued as cycle dealers on this site until about 1937 and Tesco's opened their first store here in about 1964. The original store was large before the era of out of town hypermarkets, and it was much extended in 1978. By current retailing standards, however, it is quite small and Tesco's describe it as a Metro store.

Sawyer's newsagent's shop at 166 Cowley Road, 10 May 1938. King George VI's visit to the RAF, Churchill's speech about the League of Nations, Lord Nuffield's million and the police hunt for a missing Oxford undergraduate dominate the national news. A large sign reminds passers-by that they can save money by shopping locally.

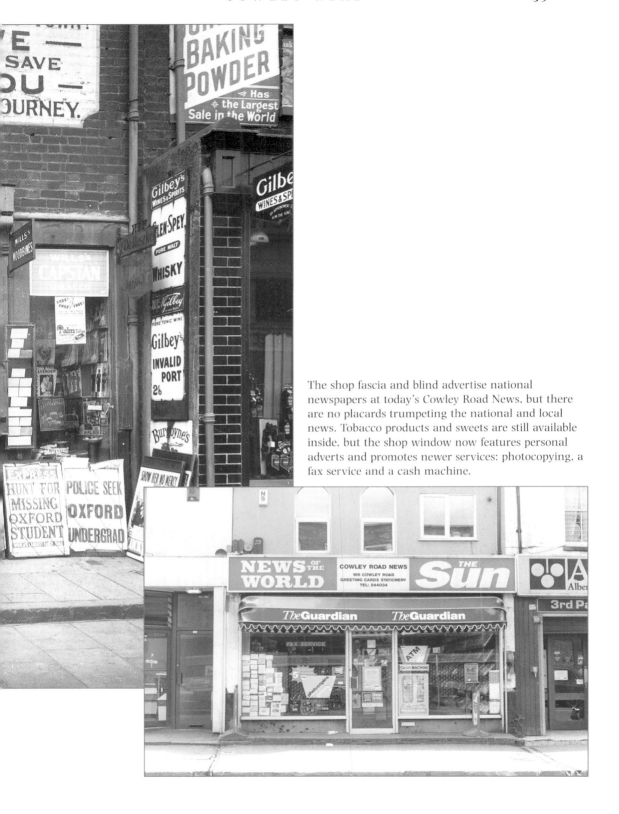

The shop fascia and blind advertise national newspapers at today's Cowley Road News, but there are no placards trumpeting the national and local news. Tobacco products and sweets are still available inside, but the shop window now features personal adverts and promotes newer services: photocopying, a fax service and a cash machine.

Buckler's fishmonger's shop at 168 Cowley Road, May 1979. Slater's, near The Plain, and Buckler's, here, wer the last Oxford examples of open-fronted shops where fish of all kinds were laid out on slabs for everyone inspection. Buckler's had been in business here since about 1908.

Ali's delicatessen has taken over Buckler's old shop, selling Lebanese savouries and specialising in vegetarian food. With the Mandarin House Chinese restaurant next door and many other outlets selling food from all over the world, modern Cowley Road is an amazingly cosmopolitan place.

Celebrating Queen Victoria's Diamond Jubilee at the Ampney Cottage, 1897. Flags adorn the creeper-clad frontage of this pub on the corner of Bullingdon Road. The Ampney Cottage was opened for business in about 1870, and the name probably recalled the Wiltshire origins of an early licensee.

Renamed the Hobgoblin by the Wychwood Brewery, the former Ampney Cottage has lost its front garden and abandoned its original corner entrance. Despite the loss of growing space on the ground, containers at first floor level maintain the pub's tradition of luxuriant planting.

Cowley Road, in sombre wartime mood, looking back towards the city centre from Bullingdon Road, April 1941. Petrol rationing had reduced the flow of traffic that had led to the installation of an experimental pedestrian-operated crossing in 1936. Instead, most shoppers are using bicycles or 'Shanks's Pony'. (*Newsquest (Oxfordshire) Ltd*)

More cars than shoppers are evident in today's view, and there is less scope to prop your bike against the pavement while dashing in to buy something. On the right, beyond Chapel Street, the decidedly functional Tesco store dominates Cowley Road with Boots the Chemist striving to be seen next door.

Pedestrians outside Home Linens await their chance to cross Cowley Road near Chapel Street, July 1968. Behind the parked Hillman Minx the ironmonger's, Shergolds, had recently taken over premises still advertised on the chimneystack as 'Butlers ironmongery, china and glass stores'. Butlers had traded as ironmongers at this site since the mid-1920s.

Cowley Road east of Chapel Street has changed much less and even the old Butlers sign, now very faded, is still there. Double yellow lines restrict parking in the foreground and a refuge in the centre of the road makes crossing at this point slightly easier perhaps than it was in the late 1960s.

The Ancient Order of Foresters parade their banner proclaiming 'Help in Time of Need' at the corner of East Avenue, July 1897. Friendly Societies like this provided vital health insurance in return for weekly payments from members in the days before national schemes were introduced. Bartholomew Fortescue's nursery occupied the glass houses behind the banner.

A rather forlorn-looking Crown House occupies the site of Fortescue's Nursery and the creeper-clad 193 Cowley Road. Thanks to the National Health Service, the age of the sick club is long gone, but so is the time when people could stand around in the middle of Cowley Road listening to a band.

A light blue and white Ford Escort belonging to the new Thames Valley police force stands beside the kerb near the East Oxford police station, July 1968. Across Cowley Road, three tall Victorian villas stand next to the huge Oxford and District Co-op store that had been built in 1909 to cater for the growing local population.

The former Co-op emporium is now shared by Supatile and the Zodiac Club, the latter an important part of the Oxford music scene. On the left, flats with bold horizontal stripes of brickwork have filled a gap in front of what used to be the engineering department of the Oxford College of Further Education.

Soldiers of the Oxfordshire and Buckinghamshire Light Infantry march past the workhouse grounds on their way to the railway station, May 1897. Fruit and vegetables for workhouse inmates were grown in the extensive gardens behind the hedge and a men's urinal.
A signboard on the left announces the office of local builders, Organ Bros, and, in the distance, washing billows in the gardens of houses in Divinity Road.

Cars take the place of marching men as motorists edge their way towards the city centre watched by a hopeful bus user. Across the road, the white building is the former East Oxford police station and the brick public conveniences beyond it are successors to the urinal. The trees mark the boundary of Manzil Gardens, a park on the fringe of the old workhouse site.

A few soldiers and a Bullnose Morris block the approach road to the Oxford workhouse, *c.* 1915. The workhouse was built in 1864 to replace an older one in what is now Wellington Square; if funds had ever permitted, a clock would have graced its ornamental tower. During the First World War the workhouse became part of the Third Southern General Hospital and military casualties ousted the poor.

The workhouse approach road is now Manzil Way, named in 1989 after the Hindi and Urdu word for destiny. From 1948 to 1980 Cowley Road Hospital, well respected for its geriatric work, occupied the buildings of the former workhouse, but the site was cleared in 1986. East Oxford Health Centre (left) and the Manzil Resource Centre have taken over part of the workhouse garden.

Convalescent soldiers loiter in front of the workhouse, *c.* 1915. The presence in Oxford of so many young men with time on their hands proved dangerously attractive to local womenfolk, and the city police force appointed its first woman constable in 1917 to help control a feminine invasion.

Retained trees provide the chief link with the past; a few leaves are visible (top left). Cowley Road Hospital was demolished in 1986, but the kerb in front of the building can still be seen while the new Central Oxford Mosque is being built here. Beyond Manzil Way, two-storey houses of patterned brick in a neo-Victorian style are typical of the housing that now occupies much of the hospital site.

Peaceful Divinity Road, *c.* 1907, when the sender of this card trusted that she would find Miss Burrows 'better when I come up tomorrow'. The Oxford Industrial and Provident Land and Building Society bought this attractive sloping site in 1890, and houses occupied most of the plots within a few years.

Creeper-clad frontages are now bare and iron railings were removed for salvage in the Second World War, but the buildings have changed little. Divinity Road was linked to Warneford Lane and so to Headington in the 1930s. With increasing traffic this through road has now become a mixed blessing for local residents.

Oxford workhouse and Divinity Road from the tower of SS Mary's and John's church, 1895. The workhouse infirmary is visible at the rear of the site with the chapel to its right; the background of trees marks the extent of the Morrell family's South Park estate. Organ Bros ran a builder's merchant business in the foreground, and on the left, George Longhurst, painter and decorator, had a workshop behind 213 Cowley Road.

The houses in the foreground were added in the early 1900s and a Londis store now occupies Organ's site. The disappearance of the workhouse is the biggest single change, although the chapel, shorn of its turret, is now the Asian Community Cultural Centre. The background is still remarkably wooded thanks to the retention of South Park as a public park since 1932.

Oxford buses at the Southfield Road bus stop, *c.* 1916. The tramlines in the foreground are a visible reminder of the horse tram service which operated a service (no. 1) between Cowley Road and the stations from 1881 to 1914. The young motor manufacturer, W.R. Morris, had forced the local tramways company to provide a modern bus service by introducing his own fleet of buses in December 1913. The Littlemore service, via Cowley, was launched in 1916.

The no. 5 bus passes the end of Southfield Road on its way to Cowley and Blackbird Leys. The estate agent, Oliver James, occupies 251 Cowley Road, premises that were Albert Morse's draper's shop for almost half a century from about 1922 to 1970.

A cricket match in progress at the Magdalen Ground, showing the uninterrupted view across Cowley Field to the spires of Oxford, *c.* 1820. The cricket ground was formed on open land in the early nineteenth century for players from Magdalen College choir school, and it became the home of university cricket. The Varsity cricket match was played here in 1829 and the ground was the venue for the university's first athletics meeting in 1860.

Cricket Road looking towards Magdalen Road with just a glimpse of the tower of SS Mary's and John's church. Oxford University Cricket Club left the Magdalen Ground for its new home in the University Parks in 1881 and allotments took over the site. These semi-detached houses form part of an estate built by the Oxford firm, N. Moss & Son, in 1931.

The rural oasis of Bartlemas in 1908, showing, from left to right, the farmhouse, the almshouses and the medieval chapel. Originating as a remote leper hospital in the early twelfth century, Bartlemas became the property of Oriel College in 1328, providing scholars with a refuge 'in times of pestilential sickness'. The almshouses were built in 1649 on the site of buildings destroyed in the Civil War.

Allotments provide the foreground for the buildings of Bartlemas, which are now well-hidden by trees and shrubs. This is still a remarkably peaceful spot, just a few paces from a busy road and a bingo hall in the former Regal cinema.

Bartlemas chapel in about 1880, when the fourteenth-century building was reduced to the status of a farm building and timber store for Bartlemas Farm. Photographs of the interior taken in about 1900 show a decayed rood screen, a dirt floor and a wooden ladder suspended from one wall.

The restored chapel in its present setting in the private garden of Bartlemas House, the former almshouses. Restoration was carried out in 1913; the work included restoring the traceried windows to their original length. The chapel has been used for occasional services since then and a Russian Orthodox congregation worshipped here between 1941 and 1949.

The barn and other outbuildings of Southfield Farm, September 1912. Approached by a long, narrow lane from Cowley Road, Southfield Farm was even more detached than Bartlemas from the burgeoning suburb of East Oxford. The property belonged to Magdalen College, and twentieth-century residents at the farmhouse included William Margetts, an Oxford tailor, and Henry Pether, a retired farmer from Bartlemas Farm.

East Oxford finally caught up with Southfield House in 1973 when the Southfield Park flats replaced the old farmhouse and its outbuildings. The development provided more than 200 flats in 11 blocks on this attractive elevated site, which still seems far removed from the hectic Cowley Road.

Cowley Road near the corner of Kenilworth Road, 1910s. These two- and three-storeyed houses were built in the 1900s and originally offered their residents fine views across open land towards Iffley and the River Thames.

The views are now across a much wider Cowley Road to a 1930s housing estate. The houses are essentially unchanged, but they have lost their boundary hedges and only the odd gate pier survives from the unusual wooden gates. Modern street lighting is on a massive scale when compared with the little gas lamp.

Looking back towards SS Mary's and John's church as a milkman pushes his cart towards Cowley, 1917. Telephone wires and a tall sewer ventilation pipe were recent urban intrusions, but the muddy road and footpath were still an echo of country life. The prominent corrugated-iron shed on the right was part of Henry Taunt's photographic works.

A much widened tarmac road has put paid to the mud, and Glanville Road on the extreme right took up the space occupied by the hedge in the 1920s. Beyond the prominent car park sign for the Majestic Wine Warehouse, there is a row of two-storey council houses built in the 1930s. To the left of R. Bullock's coach, N. Moss & Son built an estate of semi-detached houses on previously undeveloped land in 1933–4.

Cowley Road recreation ground, showing shepherd Wing with his sheepdog and the flock of sheep that kept the grass cut, 1901. The City Council leased this site from Christ Church in 1892 to provide East Oxford's first official recreation ground. The Oxford photographer, Henry Taunt (1842–1922), lived at Rivera, the two-gabled house in the background.

To some local annoyance, N. Moss & Son bought the recreation ground site from Christ Church in 1932 and submitted plans for a housing estate there. This little playground was the eventual compromise, located between Moss's estate on the left and the earlier council estate on the right. It was intended for children up to fourteen who could only use it for unorganised games, not football or cricket.

Rivera, *c.* 1900, showing the bearded Henry Taunt with his arm on the gate chatting to a visitor or passer-by; at the back of the house a workman poses on a tall ladder. Taunt acquired this house in the 1880s and named it after his beloved River Thames. He built workshops and sheds in the grounds and concentrated his business here from about 1906 until his death in 1922.

City of Oxford Motor Services Ltd built their bus garage next to Taunt's old house in 1924. Robbed of all its land the building has remarkably survived as offices. Now it is threatened by a housing scheme that is planned for the site of the bus garage.

The 'White City' of council houses which Taunt photographed nearly opposite his house in August 1921. This estate was one of the City Council's first responses to the Housing Act of 1919, and its cottage-style homes were designed by a panel of Oxford architects. The roads were named after famous poets, Milton, Morris and Shelley.

The estate today from the corner of Shelley Road. The houses lost their attractive, but no doubt draughty, casement windows in the 1980s, and many are now privately owned; as a result, houses and gardens have become quite varied where once every property looked much the same.

# 3

# *Iffley Road to Rose Hill*

King of Prussia, Rose Hill, *c.* 1910.

Milk delivery in progress outside creeper-clad villas at the beginning of Iffley Road, 1900s. These houses were built in the 1850s and 1860s, but trees planted opposite on Christ Church land gradually robbed them of splendid views across the Thames Valley towards Hinksey Hill. Respectable by day, Victorian Iffley Road took on a different character at night when prostitutes, picturesquely described as 'nymphs of the pavement', solicited in dark corners.

The brick façades are now revealed and two houses have been heightened to provide more space. Most railings were removed for salvage during the war, but at the house on the left they survived because they protected a semi-basement. Full of glorious architectural variety, the Iffley Road frontage achieved Conservation Area status in 1977.

Iffley Road from the corner of Temple Street, 1900s. Brick houses, mostly covered in creepers, stretch away towards a distant, very tall block, known originally as Carlton Terrace, built in about 1866 on the corner of James Street. Most villas and groups of houses at first had house names that not only conveyed status, but were also essential for postal deliveries before the road was properly numbered.

Trees and shrubs obscure some properties, but the only substantial change is a small block of flats, picked out by two white windows, that was built in 1973. The former Carlton Terrace has been converted into student housing for Queen's College and all its chimney-stacks have been removed.

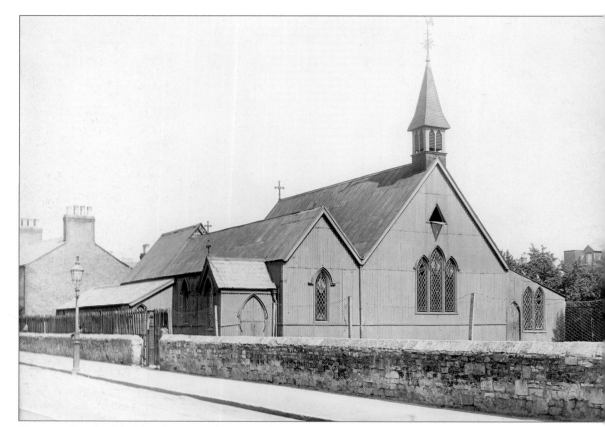

The iron church of St John the Evangelist in Stockmore Street, *c.* 1890. This mission church was built by the vicar of Cowley, the Revd Richard Benson, in 1859 to serve the fast-growing suburb of East Oxford. Benson became the first vicar of Cowley St John in 1869 and concentrated his considerable energies on the parish. Worshippers at the iron church were sometimes disturbed by local lads who peppered the roof with stones.

These cottage-style council houses occupied the site of the iron church in 1921. The opening of St John the Evangelist church in Iffley Road in 1896 made the 'temporary' iron church redundant at last, and rescued worshippers from a building that leaked like a sieve when it rained; the old church was pulled down in the same year.

Peaceful Marston Street, looking past the Swan pub towards Cowley Road, 1900s. Marston Street was laid out in the 1850s by the National Freehold Land Society and displays great architectural variety, constrained only by the Society's insistence on a building line. The beacon-like premises of the Cowley Fathers soar above the two- and three-storeyed houses. (*Jeremy Daniel*)

The Swan is now the Oxford Blue. On the right an extra house, no. 31, was slotted in during the 1920s. Further on, the street retains all its varied charm, although parked cars make this less easy to appreciate.

The Mission House of the Cowley Fathers, or the Society of St John the Evangelist, in September 1915. The Revd Richard Benson, then vicar of Cowley St John, founded the society in 1866 as a religious community within the Church of England to spread the gospel both locally and throughout the world. The striking Mission House was built in 1868 with its chapel at the very top of the building.

The last Cowley Fathers left the Mission House in 1980 and St Stephen's House, an Anglican theological college attached to the university, now occupies the extensive buildings. The chapel windows remain intact, but the pointed Gothic windows of the Mission House were unfortunately replaced in the 1960s.

A priestly procession through the Mission House vegetable garden to the dedication service of the new St John the Evangelist church in Iffley Road, May 1896. Cowley St John Girls' School stands next to the Mission House and the rear elevation of the Cowley Road Congregational church is visible away to the right.

These Italianate buildings with tiled roofs and rendered walls were a major extension to the Mission House, supplanting the vegetable garden in 1901. Only the side elevation of the old Mission House is now visible from the cloister garden. Neither the girls' school nor the Congregational church has survived.

Pigott's sausage factory in Denmark Street, *c.* 1910. Pigott's were one of the city's foremost butchers at this time with a large shop in the Covered Market, and they were noted for their Oxford sausages. The street name recalls a war between Denmark and Prussia in 1864, at the time when this area was being laid out.

Sausage making has given way to motorcycle repairs in Denmark Street today. Pigott's remained in business here until about 1937, and only disappeared from the Covered Market in about 1939.

Iffley Road, looking towards James Street from the corner of Bullingdon Road, July 1968. The Fir Tree Tavern occupied this prominent corner site by about 1869, and trade was brisk enough to require a ground-floor extension to the bar in 1901. Beyond the pub tall brick villas strain for views over the Thames Valley.

Traffic edges past road works outside the former Fir Tree, now more festive-looking and renamed the Old Ale House. The view is little changed, but it might have been so different. If the Eastwyke Farm road proposed in 1968 had ever been built, an urban motorway would have crossed Iffley Road at this point.

Newly built Stratford Street, looking towards Jackdaw Lane, 1910s. Development of the land south-west of Iffley Road only began in the 1880s, and house building in Stratford Street started in the late 1900s. The street includes some characteristic Oxford terraced houses with downstairs bay windows, but many houses have bays on both floors, providing larger and brighter front bedrooms. (*Jeremy Daniel*)

Parked cars fill the street and its appearance has been softened by trees and shrubs in front gardens. Television aerials and telephone lines are part of a changed world that early Stratford Street residents would not have anticipated.

The Co-op has had to rationalise its branches over the years, and the Hurst Street shop closed in about 1967. D. Parchment & Co. later opened a print showroom here, but now the building houses Betty and Sheila Robbins's theatrical and fancy-dress hire business.

Iffley Road looking north-west from the corner of Chester Street, *c.* 1905. Tall Gothic villas on the right beyond Aston Street, dating from the 1880s, have had their views restricted by later properties on the left. The young lime trees flourishing on the pavement were planted in the 1890s following a campaign to beautify the city's main roads.

Not all the pavement trees survived early vandalism or disease, but some have flourished and grown to maturity. Together with a few specimen trees in front gardens, they add a further dimension to the attractiveness of Iffley Road at this point.

A moment in time is frozen by the camera outside 287 and 287a Iffley Road in 1957. A mother and her son are distracted while a little girl, no doubt with sweets on her mind, strides purposefully towards Hill's post office. Next door, Burton's Dairy had taken over Stratford's fishmonger's shop to experiment with the modern concept of self-service shopping.

The shop blinds at the Globe Newsagents and Donnington Post Office now advertise the *Guardian* and the universal drink Coca-Cola. The shop has expanded into Burton's where a ramped entrance admits prams and wheelchairs. The pillar box has survived, but British Telecom replaced the old K6 phone box in the 1980s.

A grim day in Iffley Road, looking down towards Iffley Turn from the junction with Donnington Lane, 1924. Behind the fence, allotments occupy all the land on the left down to the Boundary Brook. Trees on the right mark the boundary of Freelands, a villa set well back from the road, and there is a distant glimpse of newly built council houses in Freelands Road.

Trees are still a dominant feature in this view, but they mask considerable development. With the building of Donnington Bridge in 1962, Donnington Lane became part of a busy through route to South Oxford and it was renamed Donnington Bridge Road. Beyond the traffic lights flats are set back on the site of Freelands and houses line both sides of Iffley Road.

A new life for the old Allied Arms pub: the Oxford and District Co-operative Society's Rose Hill store, 1937. When Morrell's Oxford Brewery Ltd opened their new pub, the society seized the opportunity to convert the old building into a shop to serve nearby private housing estates at Courtland Road and Westbury Crescent and the Rose Hill council estate begun in 1934.

The Oxford, Swindon and Gloucester Co-op's Swift Shop on the same site at Rose Hill today. The shop is right next to Humphris's garage where shoppers are tempted by a forecourt display of Nissan cars.

Landlord Mr James with his wife, two children and regular customers outside the King of Prussia pub at Rose Hill, *c.* 1910. The pub is first recorded in 1809, and it was probably named after Frederick William III, one of the allied sovereigns who visited Oxford in triumph in 1814 when Napoleon was exiled in Elba and apparently defeated.

The present King of Prussia pub, rebuilt in 1935, with its original name recently restored. The pub's name was changed to the Allied Arms in 1914 because of anti-German feeling, and in the late 1930s its sign showed sporting rather than military allies. Between 1977 and 1996 it was called the Ox.

A lone Hillman Minx negotiates the Rose Hill roundabout, September 1966. The Eastern Bypass extension between here and the Heyford Hill roundabout opened in September 1965 and completed the Oxford ring road some thirty-five years after work began on the first section between Hinksey Hill and Botley. One effect in East Oxford was to take away much of the through traffic between Oxford and Henley which had always used Iffley Road and Rose Hill.

Busier times at the Rose Hill roundabout, which now has traffic lights to control the flow. The houses in the background have disappeared behind an earthen mound designed to minimise noise pollution from the ring road.

# 4

# *Oxford Road to Pressed Steel*

Cowley villagers, Oxford Road, in the 1900s.

Rival conversations in Oxford Road at the corner of Marsh Lane, 1930s. The Exeter Hall is first mentioned in 1875, and the present building was built between the wars in the garden of the original pub. The name probably recalls the Exeter College cricket ground that occupied part of Cowley Marsh in the nineteenth century.

*Opposite, below*: Oxford Road is a much busier thoroughfare and a pelican crossing has been installed to make it safe to cross. The Exeter Hall still flourishes and the houses beyond the pub are little changed. The hedge and trees on the right marking the boundary of the Elder Stubbs allotments give the modern view a more rural aspect.

Pile, or Oxford, Road in muddy conditions, *c.* 1910. The old name, unsurprisingly abandoned in about 1920, derived from the fact that the road across Cowley Marsh had been supported on wooden piles. Terraced properties and a few individual houses were built here from the 1890s, bringing the suburbs ever closer to Cowley village.

A neater and urbanised Oxford Road with smooth road and pavements and the inevitable road markings. Most of the houses have always remained purely residential, but local demand and passing traffic probably encouraged one or two enterprising folk to open shops and use their front gardens as forecourts.

A lone cyclist poses for the photographer in Oxford Road, August 1912. Behind an area of rough ground and a recently installed telephone pole, a row of identical terraced houses stands primly behind low walls and iron railings.

The terraced houses, minus their iron railings, survive and the rough grass has given way to an extremely wide pavement which provides parking space for customers of the Motorists' Discount Centre. Houses have supplanted the tree on the left and there is a large garage and filling station just round the corner.

An imposing stone house, formerly The Elms, but known latterly as 170–2 Oxford Road, *c.* 1960. Situated at the foot of the slope where Oxford Road rises towards Temple Road, the building perhaps dated back to the eighteenth century. Members of the Doubleday family lived there in the early twentieth century, and Miss Knott, a teacher at St Christopher's School, was a later resident at no. 170.

Cowley police station was built on the site in 1966, just two years before the Oxford City Police were amalgamated with other local forces to form the Thames Valley Police. Decidedly Brutalist in style, the new building provided a base for 100 police officers in the Cowley Division. Facilities included sleeping accommodation for up to six officers and six centrally heated cells, the two women's cells even having foam mattresses.

The Stocks Tree, an elm tree on the corner of Oxford Road, shortly before it was felled in 1907. A tattered notice on the tree trunk advises travellers to turn left into Temple Road for the Church Army Press. White's barn is in the shade beyond the tree with the old Original Swan opposite; the Waggon and Horses can be seen in the distance on the far corner of Between Towns Road.

Oxford Road was widened on the northeast side beyond Temple Road in the 1930s and the Original Swan, partially hidden by the van, was rebuilt on the site of the Waggon and Horses in about 1910.

A goodly turnout of Cowley villagers gathers in Oxford Road above the Stocks Tree, 1900s. Behind the baker, Mr Lamburn, in his trap, Oxford Road can be seen curving away downhill towards the city. The barn belonging to White's Farm is to the right of the group.

The police would soon be out to move along obstructive folk blocking Oxford Road today. The road now curves away between the police station and the United Reformed church of 1929–30 before passing shops and houses built in the 1930s.

Oxford Road at the junction with Between Towns Road, 1968. The Village House, a former private house on the corner, had become the first home of the Cowley Workers' Club, opening on 31 May 1929. Further on, the brick-built 1930s block was occupied by W.F. Beechey, the pram dealer, Meredith's shoe shop, Silk's the grocers and Dunford's the butchers.

Cedar Court, a development of flats built in 1996, now occupies the site. The old properties were pulled down in 1969, and the site remained empty for so long that many local people must have despaired of ever seeing anything built there.

Jim and Sarah White with their children, Steven, Flo and Win, outside the Waggon and Horses pub, *c*. 1900. The first-floor window box alongside the Hall's Oxford Brewery sign is echoed by another on the adjoining house where Mr White had his baker's shop.

In rationalising mood, Hall's built a new Original Swan pub on the site of the Waggon and Horses in about 1910. The pub flourished between the wars, and it was enlarged to meet demand from the nearby Cowley Works and the fast-growing suburb. The pub is still so much a part of the local scene that bus passengers wanting the nearby stop in Between Towns Road always ask for the Swan.

John Payne, coachman to Col. Lindsay, poses outside the gates of Cowley Manor House, 1890s. Senior staff at the Oxford Military College made the manor house their home from 1876 until financial problems led to the closure of the college in 1896. Col. Lindsay was Secretary to the college in the early 1890s and lived locally at a house called Elmsthorpe.

The gates of Cowley Manor House have survived, but they were set further back when Oxford Road was widened in the 1930s.

Cowley Manor House basks in the sun while a dog takes advantage of the shade, *c.* 1870. The house was built in about 1680 and later became part of Cowley College, a diocesan school established here in 1839. Its façade was quite symmetrical with a large gable either side of the central door and massive projecting chimney stacks at each end of the façade.

A glimpse of the Manor House site beneath the spreading branches of a tree. William Morris acquired the Manor House when he bought the former Military College buildings as a car factory in 1912. It was demolished as a dangerous structure in 1957, and a new building was erected on the site during the conversion of the Nuffield Press buildings into Morris Oxford Place in 1998.

Cowley College buildings, looking towards Hollow Way from the Manor House garden, *c.* 1870. The three-storey block on the corner was built as classrooms and dormitories in 1852, and the single-storey chapel, designed by the Oxford architect Edward Bruton, was added in 1870.

Morris Oxford Place, an ingenious conversion of former Cowley College, Military College and Nuffield Press buildings into prestige apartments, was completed in 1999. Part of the new building on the Manor House site is visible on the left, and the photographs seem to show that the chapel was, at some stage, realigned with the corner block.

Hollow Way, looking north from the junction with Garsington Road, on a rainy day in June 1968. The Morris Oxford Press, later the Nuffield Press, took over the original Morris works in 1925 as purpose-built car factories spread along Garsington Road, but Lord Nuffield kept his office in the corner building. Percy Church established his garage beyond the Nuffield Press in about 1934.

Hollow Way now features the restored frontage of the old Morris works and a new building in the spirit of T.G. Jackson's work for the Oxford Military College. Opposite, the Post Office's Oxford sorting office takes up part of the site of the old Morris Motors North Works, cleared in 1993–4. A reconstruction of Lord Nuffield's office can now be seen at the British Motor Heritage Museum in Gaydon.

Spectators at a parade in the quadrangle of the Oxford Military College to mark the visit of the Duke of Cambridge on 10 June 1890. The Military College was founded in 1876 and aimed to prepare boys for commissions in the services. The architect, T.G. Jackson, produced ambitious plans for a huge quad, but only parts of the south range, seen here, and the east range were ever built; the little building on the right was a laboratory added in 1882.

Residents' cars fill Morris Oxford Place and there is a glimpse of the former St Luke's church, now Oxfordshire Record Office, in the background. The Oxford Military College failed in 1896 and its buildings later became part of the Nuffield Press until 1995. They were converted to residential use in 1999, but the old laboratory, used for many years as a practice room by Morris Motors Band, was demolished.

Gate no. 10, the Garsington Road entrance to the Service and Repair Departments of Morris Motors Ltd, 1930s. The Morris works began to spread on to the open land across Hollow Way in 1919 and expanded rapidly towards the Poor Law school as vehicle production soared in the 1920s. The lone gas lamp seems like a relic from another age beside the huge industrial buildings and prominent boiler-house chimney.

Part of the Oxford Business Park in Garsington Road, showing the nursery, kidsunlimited and part of the Travel Inn. In the postwar British Motor Corporation and British Leyland years, Cowley's Assembly Plant was based here in the North Works. Following the decision to rationalise production on the Pressed Steel site, the former Morris factories were cleared in 1993–4 and the site was transformed into a modern business park.

Approaching the Cowley works along the Eastern bypass in June 1967. Space was left in the 1930s for a bypass to be driven between the Morris works on the left and the Pressed Steel Co. factory on the right, but the road was not built until 1961. The bridge across the bypass was built in 1954 to convey motor bodies from the Body Plant to the Assembly Plant and save large numbers of lorry movements between the sites.

With the loss of many established landmarks, including the conveyor bridge and factory chimneys, a totally different Cowley now exists. A bridge now carries the Eastern bypass over Garsington Road, and the Oxford Business Park is filling the site of the North and South Works. BMW has invested substantially in the old Pressed Steel site, which is now producing the new Mini.

The homeward dash from Pressed Steel in 1950 at a time when rush hour in Cowley meant an alarming number of bikes in the streets. The factory buildings are still clearly painted in wartime camouflage and railway wagons beneath the canopy of 'A' Building are evidence of the extensive internal rail network which served the site.

Customary queues at the traffic-light controlled roundabout beneath the Eastern bypass flyover. Modern cladding has updated 'A' Building, and the old Pressed Steel office building is visible in the background. The factory's internal rail system is no more, but Cowley still has a rail freight terminal off Watlington Road.

The strikingly modern office building erected for the Pressed Steel Co. in 1936. Within 10 years of its foundation, the firm was employing over 3,000 people and the figure rose to 9,000 by 1939; just before the war Pressed Steel was producing 700 car bodies a day.

The BMW offices today, hemmed in by the southbound slip road from the Eastern bypass. First-floor windows have considerably altered the look of the building and the louvred upper section of the central tower has been filled in to house a clock.

A man pauses beside Barracks Lane at the foot of Lye Hill, 1914. Beyond the stile a footpath rises past a hedgerow filled with elms. The photographer, Henry Taunt, describes it as continuing across Sand Hill, past a quarry used for the building of Cowley Barracks and on to Headington Moor.

A woman out for a stroll stops at the same point today. Barracks Lane is more thickly wooded and Cowley's remaining meadows are no longer mown for hay or grazed by sheep. Fencing on the left marks the boundary of Oxford School's playing fields, and the footpath now continues across Southfield Golf Course to the Boundary Brook nature reserve, a narrow tongue of undeveloped land between Lye Valley and the Churchill Hospital.

Paddling on a hot summer day, July 1914. Children take advantage of the old sheep-washing place on the Boundary Brook in Barracks Lane. Beyond the happy group the lane curves away to the left towards Sand Hill and the Horspath Road.

Barracks Lane is now less of an informal children's playground, but it provides cyclists and pedestrians with a quiet alternative to the Cowley and Oxford roads. The Boundary Brook ceased to be the boundary between the city and Cowley in 1929, but it still ripples along quite merrily at this point behind all the vegetation.

A man and his dog on the portion of Barracks Lane known as Sand Hill, or Sandy Lane, July 1914. The lane rises towards Horspath Road from here, passing the site of Bullingdon Castle, a folly built in the nineteenth century that was occupied by the Windows family until the 1860s.

This part of Barracks Lane was upgraded to a road in 1973 when houses were built on undeveloped land between here and Crescent Road, and two new streets, Turner's Close and Leafield Road, were formed. A section of rubble walling at the corner of the Morris Motors sports ground still survives beyond these houses as a possible last link with Bullingdon Castle.

Crescent Road from part of the golf course on Cowley Marsh, *c.* 1900. Crescent Road and Junction Road were laid out by the British Land Company in 1864 following the success of earlier estates in East Oxford, but the site was quite remote at this time and development was slow. College cricket grounds occupied much of Cowley Marsh in the nineteenth century, and golfers took over this area in about 1875.

A huge shed at the City Council's Marsh Lane depot obscures much of Crescent Road and Temple Cowley. The former Salesian College is visible on the left and the tower of St Luke's church, built in 1938, can be seen on the right. Although the golf course moved to the nearby Southfield course in 1923 and development has encroached on to the fringes of Cowley Marsh, a large area is still used for recreation.

Muddy conditions in Crescent Road, *c.* 1910. Building byelaws, reinforced by public protest, brought effective drainage and black brick pavements to most suburban streets in Oxford, but Cowley remained outside the city, and mud was a predictable aspect of country life.

Today's road surface and pavements in Crescent Road may be patched, but at least they are weatherproof. The Victorian terraced houses on the left have survived, but on the right some properties have given way to more modern houses, set back further from the road.

The Betoy Ltd factory at the foot of Crescent Road, *c. 1970*. Betoy's made teddy bears here, but the building was originally the parish gymnasium founded in 1892 by the Revd T.J. Dyson, Principal of Wycliffe Hall, and Cowley's irrepressible vicar, the Revd George Moore. The Aslin Blind Co. later took over the building to make paper blinds 'as good as linen ones'.

Shorn of its chimney, Betoy's old factory is now the Oxford Print and Copy Centre for Parchment's, a local printing business established in the 1960s. The building was badly damaged by serious fires in the 1920s and again in 1978, and was restored on both occasions.

The Franciscan College in Crescent Road, *c.* 1910. An Anglican boarding school, St Kenelm's College commissioned this handsome building from the Oxford architect, Harry Wilkinson Moore, in 1880. The school failed in about 1903 and the Franciscans took over the premises in 1906.

The building is now divided into flats as Salesian House, and beyond the wall, part of the grounds have been developed as Salesian Gardens. The Salesian Order took over the building in 1921 after the Franciscans moved to Iffley Road, and it formed the nucleus of the Salesian College, a Roman Catholic day and boarding school, until the 1970s. After a prolonged period of neglect the building was restored, and the site was developed in 1992.

Mrs Honour and her daughter, Daisy, outside the shop at the corner of Crescent Road and Temple Road, *c.* 1895. The building to the right was the bakery attached to the shop. The shop is liberally decorated with advertisements for popular products: Sunlight and Venus Soaps, Cadbury's Cocoa, Fry's Chocolate and Salmon's Reading Teas.

The Corner Stores are now sadly boarded up, one of the many victims of our changing lifestyles and the retailing revolution. The redundant chimney-stack has gone and just two upstairs sash windows have been retained on the Crescent Road elevation. The little garden next to the former bakery has become a parking place.

A quiet day in Temple Road, 1912. Stepped rows of Victorian terraced houses recede down the hill, each hous having its own front flower garden protected by a low brick wall and railings. In complete contrast, tree bordering an orchard still overhang the other side of the road.

A narrowing of the roac and a speed hump bear witness to efforts to slow motorists down in this residential area. On the right, 53 Temple Road has come out from behind its creeper and now presents a rendere frontage to the world. Ornamental railings have gone and some houses lower down have sprouted loft conversions.

A temporary blockage in Temple Road as schoolchildren go home for lunch, 11 March 1958. On the right, a rubble stone outbuilding behind 76 Temple Road had been a small slaughterhouse for the Hedges family, butchers in the Covered Market, who lived here in the early twentieth century.

No congestion today on this corner of Temple Road, as fewer children go home to lunch these days; and double yellow lines deter parking. The outbuilding behind no. 76 has made way for a garden.

The Factory in the Fields

A horse and cart outside the Church Army Press, Temple Road, 1900s. The Church Army Press, founded in London in 1882, moved its printing office to Cowley in 1903, and over sixty employees were working here by 1913. The Cricketers' pub is visible on the left and the lady on the pavement with her family has been identified as Mrs Hedges.

The retained buildings of the Church Army Press face a rebuilt Cricketers' pub of the 1930s across Temple Road. The Church Army Press closed down in the 1980s and its premises, still looking very much as they did a century ago, were converted to residential use in 1989. In the distance, Silkdale Close replaced Rock House, home of the Hurst family of Cowley, in the 1960s.

A Co-op van approaches Hollow Way from Horspath Road, *c.* 1931. The area is clearly changing fast as the growth of the motor industry generates a huge demand for new housing. Horspath Road is being widened and improved and semi-detached houses built by the Coventry firm Ives & Rushby can be seen in the distance.

The pavement of a widened Horspath Road shaves the corner of no. 168 Hollow Way, but the road is now a little quieter since access to the bypass was closed at the other end. The hedge on the right marks the boundary of the Horspath Road Recreation Ground, a bit of open space retained by the developers of the adjoining Sunnyside Estate.

The Hollow Way frontage to Cowley Barracks, 1907. The Regimental Depot of the Oxfordshire and Buckinghamshire Light Infantry was built in 1876. It was part of a national reorganisation of the army, and barracks of similar design with forbidding 'keeps' can be seen locally in Reading and Devizes. The development brought welcome business, but there were some fears in Oxford that the soldiers would be a corrupting influence.

New blocks have been added to the remaining buildings of the Barracks on Hollow Way, and, as Paul Kent Hall, they provide student housing for Oxford Brookes University. The Oxfordshire and Buckinghamshire Light Infantry regimental depot moved to Winchester in 1958 and the regiment merged with the Royal Green Jackets in 1966. The Post Office took over much of Cowley Barracks and demolished the keep in Hollow Way as unsafe in 1971.

The shopping parade and semi-detached houses of Wilkins Road, August 1939. Built in 1931–2, Wilkins Road was part of the Sunnyside estate, named after a house in Hollow Way that briefly became a convalescent home for women and children in 1922. The builders were Ives & Rushby of Coventry and A.E. Harris.

Wilkins Road today from the junction with Fern Hill Road. Mature front garden planting has softened the hard edges of the estate and the shops flourish, some apparently by welcoming cars on to the forecourt and others by keeping them at bay. A BT phone box has replaced one of the Post Office's K3 concrete telephone boxes.

A country ramble beside Brasenose Farm, July 1916. The walkers were perhaps wending their way slowly back to Cowley village and would make use of Horspath Driftway and a completely undeveloped Horspath Road. Brasenose Farm, in the background, dates back to the eighteenth century.

The Eastern bypass, built in 1961, is now no place for country walks or quiet botanical study. Brasenose Farm, spied through the trees, is however the base for Oxford City Council's Countryside Service, and within a few paces you can be enjoying the peaceful surroundings of Brasenose Wood and Shotover Country Park.

# 6

# *Cowley Centre to Blackbird Leys*

St James's church, Cowley, 1860s.

Between Towns Road looking towards Oxford Road, March 1953. The road had become a real mixture of residential properties and shops such as F.R. Watts, the butcher's, at no. 24 on the left; on the right, the Cowley Conservative Club stands next to St Luke's Road. In the distance the Nuffield Press occupies the former Military College, and its extension of 1931 is clearly visible. (*Newsquest (Oxfordshire) Ltd*)

The buildings of the Cowley Conservative Club, the Nuffield Press and St Luke's church have survived, through they have different uses now. However, the south-east side of Between Towns Road beyond Cowley Parish Hall has changed completely. Broadfield House, the four-storey office block, was occupied for many years by the Potato Marketing Board, and the smaller building to its left is the modern Cowley Workers' Social Club.

A moment of stillness as everyone poses for the camera in Between Towns Road, *c.* 1907. The row of Victorian terraced houses included the old Cowley Post Office, which can be picked out by the signs and notices around and above the bay window. The road curves round towards Oxford Road with the newly built Original Swan visible on the corner.

Between Towns Road was realigned in 1960–1 as part of the City Council's Cowley Centre development, and Raglan House on the corner of Barns Road now stands on the site; Raglan House and adjoining offices were built in 1982. The side elevation of Cowley Parish Hall is visible on the left.

Hockmore Street from Between Towns Road, *c. 1960*. No. 25 Hockmore Street, a formerly thatched house with a corrugated-iron roof, stands on the corner with the still thatched no. 27 in the distance beside the advertisement hoardings. Bentley & Sons newsagent's shop at no. 25a is visible beyond the bus stop, and the pub sign for the Nelson is away to the right.

The equivalent view today is this service road off Barns Road, which gives rear access to shops in The Square. Nos 1 and 2 The Square, the former Sainsbury's store in Cowley Centre, are straight ahead with the side elevation of the Barns Road Car Park on the right.

Barns Court from the Coronation Lamp in Hockmore Street, 1920s. Gas street lighting reached Cowley village in 1911, and this special lamp was erected by public subscription to commemorate the Coronation of George V. With a suitable turning space, this area later became the terminus for Cowley buses. No. 19 Hockmore Street, on the right, was half of a thatched stone building dating back to the seventeenth century.

The northern end of Barns Road was realigned in 1960–1 and service bays for 36–45 Upper Barr occupy the site. The Coronation Lamp was taken away during the redevelopment of the area and it has never been seen again.

Nos 14–18 Hockmore Street, *c.* 1936. These houses stood on a corner site next to the Carpenter's Arms pub; one resident, Old Jimmy, collected copies of *The Oxford Times* in a box truck every week and sold them around the village. Sanitary inspectors judged the properties unfit for human habitation under the terms of the Housing Act 1930, and they were demolished soon after this photograph was taken.

This long-lost corner of Hockmore Street is now beneath Radio Rentals and the Discount Shoe Zone in Pound Way. The old buildings were pulled down in April 1936 and the site remained vacant for years until the Cowley Centre development.

Ridged-up potatoes in the garden behind 35–7 and 37a Hockmore Street, *c.* 1936. These are more condemned village properties that fell short of urban sanitary standards following the incorporation of Cowley within Oxford in 1929. A glimpse of the Carpenter's Arms pub above the wooden shed provides the key to the location of these buildings in Hockmore Street.

Serried rows of shoes and shoe boxes at Shoe Express in Pound Way are a modern equivalent of the rows of potatoes. The old Hockmore Street site was again cleared in 1936, but the Carpenter's Arms opposite lasted until 1961.

Time for celebration in Hockmore Street, perhaps at the time of the Coronation of Edward VII in 1902. People stand around and the Co-op delivery man waits patiently while the photographer records the festive flags and bunting. The Victorian terraces, some set back from the pavement and others on the pavement edge, contrast with the older stone cottage beyond the tree.

Bunting stretched across Pound Way provides a faint echo with the past in the totally different environment of today's Templars Square.

Hockmore Street from the corner of Crowell Road, *c.* 1960. Nos 52–6 are delightful stone cottages dating back to the eighteenth century with tiled roofs and gabled dormers. Beyond them, the eye is led past the frontage of John Allen & Son's to a 1930s semi on the corner of Rymers Lane.

The John Allen Shopping Centre, built in 1987, occupies the site of the local engineering business, but the gable end of the works is visible beyond B&Q. It was taken down brick by brick during the demolition and rebuilt a few feet back from its original position. The old Hockmore Street houses were demolished in 1960 to make way for the new alignment of Between Towns Road.

Supporting local business, John Allen, owner of the Oxfordshire Steam Ploughing Co. Ltd, stands proudly behind his firm's fleet of Bullnose Morris cars in November 1918. Founded in 1868, the business manufactured and hired out steam ploughing equipment and other machinery and became Cowley's first major employer.

A glimpse of the rebuilt gable end and the huge B&Q store from the corner of Between Towns Road and Rymers Lane. John Allen's steam ploughs helped to prepare the sites of the Cowley factories for building in the 1920s, but the firm became noted for road-making equipment, tracked vehicles and motor scythes. Latterly Grove Allen's and crane makers, the firm continued in business until 1985.

Members of the City Council's Cowley Centre Development Committee admire the fruits of their labours in Between Towns Road, 1964. Beyond Crowell Road the new precinct is nearing completion and Hockmore Tower is up to roof level; away to the right, work is under way on the multi-storey car park. (*Newsquest (Oxfordshire) Ltd*)

The building of the John Allen Centre away to the left has made this a busy crossroads, so lights are now needed to control the traffic. This view of Cowley Centre has changed little, but a large temporary sign beyond Connell's encourages people down a pedestrian route into the revamped Templars Square.

Pound Way and Hockmore Tower, April 1973. The new Cowley Centre provided sixty-eight shops, including four department stores, to serve the growing local population and to reduce congestion in central Oxford by decentralising shopping facilities. In order to keep the centre busy outside shop hours, fifty-eight flats were provided in Hockmore Tower and twenty-three maisonettes were built above the shops in Pound Way.

The roofed-over Pound Way that was thoroughly modernised when the ageing Cowley Centre was reborn as Templars Square in 1989. From the early days in the 1960s people complained about the wind tunnel effect in Pound Way, and the creation of this climate-controlled space has been a popular feature.

Mothers and children linger happily around the fountain in The Square, *c*. 1970. Sainsbury's opened a store at Cowley Centre in 1964, but customers clearly had to run the gauntlet of majestically sprung prams before they could reach the shopping aisles. On the left, the Co-op tempted buyers with the timeless slogan 'Buy Now Pay Later'.

The north-east corner of The Square today with two market stalls and space that is sometimes used for displays and performances. The Square was also roofed over as part of the Templars Square development; a restaurant occupies part of the space. The unlit background marks the site of Sainsbury's store, which finally closed because many of its customers now travel to the firm's Heyford Hill hypermarket on the ring road.

St James's church in Cowley in the early 1860s when three local lads were sufficiently fascinated to remain still for the photographer. First recorded in 1149, the church included a late twelfth-century nave and chancel arch, and a fifteenth-century west tower. Inside, a west gallery had been added in 1824 to provide more accommodation, but by 1849 the church was judged to be too small for the growing population.

The church was extended in 1864, under the direction of the architect George Edmund Street, but the building of a north aisle and the heightening of the nave had the effect of dwarfing the church tower. Some of the old gravestones have been retained, and although St James's is now set in the centre of a large urban population, the churchyard could still be set in a country village.

The Bakers' smithy in Littlemore Road, *c.* 1900, showing, from left to right, Fred Baker, -?-, Mr Giles and George Baker. George was known as the Singing Blacksmith, because he sang while he worked, and he mended children's iron hoops free of charge. The cart on the left belonged to the local carrier, Silas Turner, who travelled into Oxford daily.

Compass Close, a development of fifteen flats, built in about 1968, stands on the site of the smithy. The Bakers continued in business here until the early 1940s as Cowley was transformed around them, and semi-detached houses were built right next door to the smithy in Littlemore Road.

Littlemore Road looking north towards Crowell Road, June 1938. Some of the semi-detached houses built in the 1930s formed a ribbon of development linking the formerly separate villages of Cowley and Littlemore. A poster on the right announces a forthcoming sale of demolition materials in nearby Cowley Road, Littlemore.

Road works are a constant between the two views, but grass verges have given way to tarmac pavements and gas street lighting is no more. On the right, a tall gable end picks out the Nuffield Arms pub, built on the corner of Bartholomew Road in about 1939.

Some of the first residents of Sandy Lane in 1958 who were protesting, rather happily it seems, about having to walk a mile and a half to Rose Hill School. The building of Blackbird Leys began in 1957 and 23–33 Sandy Lane, seen in the background, were the first houses on the estate to be occupied. (*Newsquest (Oxfordshire) Ltd*)

Cyclists, Mark and Michael Hall, take a break outside the same houses today. Blackbird Leys housed about 7,000 people by 1965, and by 1991 that figure had risen to 13,464.

A woman strides purposefully towards the shops in Blackbird Leys Road, September 1967. This parade of twelve shops was built in 1961 and included two-storey maisonettes on the upper floors accessed by open staircases. In 1967 the shops included Deltey's Supermarket, Falconer's, the chemist, and Betty's, a ladies' outfitter. Windrush Tower, completed in 1962, is away to the right.

Trees at the foot of Windrush Tower have softened the hard edges of the early view and hanging baskets decorate the tall lamp-posts. Deltey's is still on the parade and other businesses include Forbuoys the newsagent's, Lloyd's Pharmacy and Nash's Bakery. Traffic calming measures were in part a response to an outbreak of 'joy-riding', which brought the area unwelcome publicity in 1991.

Evenlode Tower from Blackbird Leys Road, March 1969. A very few cars are parked at the foot of the fifteen-storey block that was completed in 1962. Some of the buildings of Redefield School, Blackbird Leys' own secondary school, can be seen in the background and a few retained trees on the right provide a link with the old landscape before development.

Trees are gradually giving a parkland atmosphere to the grassland in the foreground, but there is still space for an impromptu game of football. Back in 1962 it was claimed that the tower blocks of Blackbird Leys 'offered modern living at its best', and with controlled ground floor access and private gardens, they have come much nearer to that ideal. Redefield School closed in 1982 and Oxford College uses the buildings for adult education classes.

# BRITAIN IN OLD PHOTOGRAPHS

### Northamptonshire

Northampton Past &
Present

### Nottinghamshire

Arnold & Bestwood:
A Second Selection
Kirkby in Ashfield:
A Second Selection
Nottinghamshire at Work
Nottingham Past & Present

### Oxfordshire

Around Abingdon
Around Didcot
Around Henley-on-Thames
Around Wheatley
Around Witney
Around Woodstock
Banbury
Banbury Past & Present
Cowley & East Oxford Past
& Present
Forgotten Thames
Garsington
Henley-on-Thames Past &
Present
Literary Oxford
Oxford
Oxfordshire at Play
Oxfordshire at School
Wantage, Faringdon & The
Vale Villages
Witney

### Shropshire

Shropshire Railways
South Shropshire
Telford

### Somerset

Chard & Ilminster

### Staffordshire

Aldridge Revisited
Kinver & Enville: A Second
Selection

Newcastle-under-Lyme Past
& Present
Pattingham & Wombourne
Stafford
Stoke-on-Trent Past &
Present

### Suffolk

Bury St Edmunds
Lowestoft Past & Present
Southwold
Stowmarket
Suffolk Transport
Suffolk at Work: A Second
Selection

### Surrey

Cheam & Belmont
Esher
Richmond
Walton upon Thames &
Weybridge

### Sussex

Around East Grinstead
Around Heathfield:
A Second Selection
Bishopstone & Seaford:
A Second Selection
Eastbourne Past & Present
High Weald: A Second
Selection
Horsham Past & Present
Lancing
Palace Pier, Brighton
RAF Tangmere
Rye & Winchelsea

### Tyne & Wear

Whitley Bay

### Warwickshire

Around Leamington Spa
Around Leamington Spa:
A Second Selection
Around Bulkington
Bedworth Past & Present
Knowle & Dorridge

Nuneaton Past & Present
Rugby: A Second Selection
Warwickshire Railways

### West Midlands

Bilston, Bradley &
Ladymoor
Birmingham Transport
Black Country Pubs
Blackheath
Cradley Heath
Cradley Heath: A Second
Selection
Darlaston, Moxley &
Bentley
Great Bridge & District
Halesowen: A Second
Selection
Ladywood
Ladywood Revisited
Lye & Wollescote
Lye & Wollescote: A Second
Selection
Northfield Past & Present
Oldbury
Rowley
Sedgley: A Fourth Selection
Smethwick
Solihull
Stourbridge, Wollaston &
Amblecote
Stourbridge, Wollaston &
Amblecote: A Second
Selection
Tipton: A Third Selection
Wednesbury
Wordsley

### Wiltshire

Around Devizes
Around Highworth
Castle Combe to
Malmesbury
Crewkerne & the Ham
Stone Villages
Marlborough: A Second
Selection
Salisbury: A Second
Selection

### Worcestershire

Worcester Past & Present

### Yorkshire

Around Hoyland
Around Hoyland: A Second
Selection
Doncaster
Huddersfield
Huddersfield: A Second
Selection
Leeds in the News
Northallerton: A Second
Selection
Pontefract
Sheffield
Shire Green, Wincobank &
Ecclesfield
Wombwell & Darfield

### Wales

Anglesey
Carmarthen & the Tywi
Valley
Chepstow & The River
Wye
Haverfordwest
Milford Haven
Upper Teifi
Welshpool

### Scotland

Annandale
Around Lochaber
Clydesdale
Musselburgh
Perth
Selkirkshire
St Andrews

### Ireland

Coleraine & the Causeway
Coast

To order any of these titles please telephone our distributor,
Haynes Publishing, on 01963 442105
For a catalogue of these and our other titles please telephone
Joanne Govier at Sutton Publishing on 01453 732423